Would You Rather
Winter Edition

Clean, Silly, and
Downright Hilarious
Brain Teasing
Questions for All Ages

Table of Contents

Introduction

Welcome to *Would You Rather Winter Edition*! Would you rather be bored all winter break or enjoy a fun book filled with crazy questions and hilarious jokes? This book was designed with kids in mind to help pass the time between holiday events and make long days at home a little more fun. Although it was written for kids, the jokes and questions in these chapters can be enjoyed with parents, teachers, and group leaders to help spread the joy. These people can teach others and encourage more kids to work their brains on the "Would you rather..." questions and riddles.

There are three sections in this book, each relating to their own holiday. The first section is all about fall and Thanksgiving with questions that will make you think and riddles that will make you laugh. It's designed to all relate back to the holiday and the activities associated with it.

The second section is filled with witty winter would-you-rathers and funny phrases you can fill in. Grab your siblings or cousins while you wait to grab presents from the Christmas tree and see who can come up with the craziest story in the Funny Phrases section.

The final section is a collection of New Year's Eve- and Day-themed brain teasers that will surely have you laughing and ready for the ball to drop at midnight. You can move through the would-you-rather questions to find out what you'd be willing to do to have a glimpse at the future, or maybe a chance to change the past.

You can bring this book with you wherever you go in the snowy seasons, or even the summertime if you want! You never know when you'll need a little extra fun or a good way to pass the time on your own. This book is perfect to move through on your own or to play with friends and siblings. If you're in a group, make sure to share the fun with anyone and everyone around you. After all, riddles and funny phrases are fun for everyone! Don't be shy to use your newly found wit to make friends and spread a little holiday cheer.

How to Play

You can move through the book at your own pace, there's no rush to finish it all once. Each chapter corresponds to a different holiday in the fall and winter season, so you can choose to only complete those sections during that time. You can also jump around to find the easiest or hardest questions or the sections you want to complete the most.

The Would You Rather... section is the first in each chapter. These silly questions are meant to make you think hard about a variety of different situations and how you might respond to them. Some of them are straightforward and might be easy, while others could be more difficult and ask you to choose between crazy options.

The next section is chock full of jokes and riddles sure to make your sides split. The answers are all listed at the end of the book, so you can stare at the words as long as you want without accidentally seeing the answer. Ponder as long as you please until you give up or figure it out, then check your answer!

The seasonal questions are designed to make you think about your most and least favorite parts of the season and holidays. They are all multiple choice with the answers listed below the questions. You can circle the answer that fits you most and then revisit them later to see if your choice changed.

Finally, funny phrases finish each chapter. This game is funniest when played with others, but can be played on your own too. Each paragraph has parts of speech in parentheses scattered throughout it. You can ask another person or make a list of your own, coming up with words that fit the part of speech requested. After you have a list created, you can read the paragraph and insert the words you've come up with to create a hilariously silly scenario.

Chapter Outlines

The chapters are set up in chronological order by holiday, starting with Thanksgiving and moving through to the New Year. The exercises are listed as mentioned above to move you from decision making to riddle solving to question answering to scenario drawing!

Starting with the would-you-rather questions helps to get your brain geared up for the critical thinking you'll need to correctly answer all the hilarious jokes in the next section. After you've had a laugh and your brain is nice and tired, you can relax a little by answering the holiday-themed multiple choice questions that give you an opportunity to reflect on what you like and dislike. Finally, the wacky word games at the end will make sure you leave the chapter on a high note because one should always leave the crowd laughing!

Bring Families Together

Some people might think joke books are just for kids, but they can be a way to bring the whole family together. Everyone can answer a funny would-you-rather question, or try their hand at a difficult riddle. Moms and dads, grandmas and grandpas, can all come up with words to smash into a silly situation.

It can also give you a way to pass the time with family instead of alone. When you have an activity, it can be easier to chat and bond while having fun. You can share the book with your cousins, friends, or even your parents to see how they would answer some of the crazy questions.

Sharing these jokes and activities can also give people a break from the year-in and year-out traditions they're used to. Spice up any holiday party with a timed riddle contest or a would-you-rather marathon! It helps families reconnect with each other and learn a little something about everyone along the way.

Finally, it gives you, the coolest kid in the room, the chance to shine and strut your stuff. You can memorize some hilarious jokes or make people laugh with your choice of would you rather. You can even use the seasonal questions as conversation starters with new friends or acquaintances. Joke books aren't just for individual fun, they're for everyone!

Chapter 1: Thanksgiving

Thanksgiving might be one of the most delicious holidays out there. A day full of feasting and family can still have some downtime, though, which is why this book can be a great resource to tide over holiday fun. The would-you-rather questions are perfect for sharing with siblings or cousins, or even the adults table if you want! If you'd rather some time to yourself, you can go through the fun fall questions in the second section to ponder your particular persuasion during the season. If you want to get the whole family laughing, you can get someone to answer the funny phrases and read it aloud for the group. The possibilities are endless!

Would You Rather...

1. Would you rather get to be on television leading the Macy's Day Parade or eat Thanksgiving dinner with a celebrity?

2. Would you rather make 100 pounds of mashed potatoes or clean all the pots that the cook used?

3. Would you rather dive into a pile of leaves, but you have to rake them up after, or rake all the leaves and not dive into the pile, but your parents give you $5?

4. Would you rather have a Thanksgiving feast for lunch or dinner?

5. Would you rather pretend to be a pilgrim at school for a month or pretend to be a turkey at school for a week?

6. Would you rather eat Thanksgiving food for breakfast, lunch, and dinner on only one day or be allowed to eat it for a week, but not on Thanksgiving day?

7. Would you rather sit next to the oldest member of your family or the youngest member of your family at Thanksgiving dinner?

8. Would you rather play football outside in the yard or play video games inside with your friends?

9. Would you rather watch Thanksgiving specials on television or read a book about the history of Thanksgiving?

10. Would you rather play a Native American or a Pilgrim in the school Thanksgiving play?

11. Would you rather reenact Thanksgiving and cook and eat food outside or cook and eat inside, but have to watch a documentary about Thanksgiving?

12. Would you rather be the first person to serve their plate, but you are limited in how much food you can take, or the last person to serve and you are unlimited in how much you can take?

13. Would you rather spend Thanksgiving with your entire family or three good friends?

14. Would you rather have Thanksgiving dinner with the president at the White House or have the president come to your house?

15. Would you rather have the best tasting Thanksgiving food, but only be allowed to take one bit, or have okay tasting Thanksgiving food and be able to eat as much as you want?

16. Would you rather dress like a turkey for a week or a Native American for a month?

17. Would you rather eat raw green beans or raw corn?

18. Would you rather work at a soup kitchen on Thanksgiving or volunteer at a homeless shelter?

19. Would you rather help your mother cook all the Thanksgiving food or make a list of 100 things you are grateful for?

20. Would you rather have turkey feathers or corn husks for hair?

21. Would you rather eat one slice of pumpkin pie with salt instead of sugar or three cans of cranberry sauce?

22. Would you rather sail on a boat to another country or farm all your own food?

23. Would you rather spend a week reliving Thanksgiving every day or go a year without Thanksgiving?

24. Would you rather talk to one member of your family for the entirety of

Thanksgiving or talk to all of your family members, but only for five minutes each?

25. Would you rather go grocery shopping with your mom for Thanksgiving ingredients or help your dad decorate the house?

26. Would you rather be a turkey on Thanksgiving or a pig on Christmas?

27. Would you rather have a hot fall and a snowy winter, or a cool fall and winter without any snow?

28. Would you rather spend the day taking care of your great grandparents or spend the day volunteering in a nursing home?

29. Would you rather go back in time to the first Thanksgiving or the first Black Friday?

30. Would you rather keep a turkey as a pet for a year, but it has to be your Thanksgiving dinner, or keep a turkey for a month and then give it away?

Thanksgiving Jokes

1. Why did the potato farmer start hammering his fields?

2. Why did the turkey cross the road?

3. What do turkeys request for dessert?

4. Why do Pilgrims wear buckles on their hats?

5. Why can't different types of birds hang out together?

6. What does a turkey do when it's injured?

7. What is a Pilgrim's favorite type of music?

8. How is a cranberry farmer similar to a pirate?

9. What instrument would a turkey play in a band?

10. Why do turkeys get so big?

11. Why don't turkeys eat on Thanksgiving?

12. What do you call a large piece of corn?

13. How did the Pilgrims show they were happy to see land?

14. What is the best thing to wear to Thanksgiving dinner?

15. What smells best on Thanksgiving?

16. Can a turkey fly higher than a skyscraper?

17. What would a Jamaican request more of in a pumpkin pie?

18. What do you call a friend who is a Pilgrim?

19. What kind of key is important for Thanksgiving, but won't open a door?

20. If you met a Pilgrim today, what would you be most impressed with?

21. Why did Thanksgiving dinner start late?

22. What does a math teacher cook for Thanksgiving?

23. What do you call a fancy dance event for turkeys?

24. Why did the Pilgrim say "God Bless America"?

25. What do you call it when a buffalo barely escapes a Native American?

Thanksgiving Questions

1. Which person is most likely to tell funny stories at Thanksgiving dinner?

   a. Grandmother

   b. Grandfather

   c. Sibling

   d. Cousin

2. What dish do you wish people would make less of for the holidays?

   a. Cranberry sauce

   b. Cabbage casserole

   c. Mac and cheese

   d. Turkey

3. What is your favorite outdoor activity in the fall?

    a. Playing in the leaves

    b. Playing football

    c. Sitting inside by the fire

    d. Shopping for new clothes

4. How many pumpkins would it take to make a pie big enough to feed your whole family?

    a. 1

    b. 2

    c. 3

    d. 4

5. Whose house is the most fun when they host Thanksgiving?

    a. Grandparents

    b. Aunt and uncle

c. Cousins

d. Siblings

6. If you had to pick just one food to eat on Thanksgiving, which would it be of the choices below?

    a. Turkey

    b. Mac and cheese

    c. Casserole

    d. Pie

7. What event would you suggest for your family to do after eating on Thanksgiving?

    a. Talent show

    b. Card tournament

    c. Singing contest

    d. Football game

8. If you could hold one of the below balloons in the Macy's Day Parade, which would it be?

    a. Pikachu

    b. Red Power Ranger

    c. Pillsbury Doughboy

    d. The Grinch

9. What is your favorite fall activity?

    a. Football

    b. Family gatherings

    c. Thanksgiving dinner

    d. Sipping cider

10. If you could pick one thing to do every day for a week, what would it be?

    a. Walking in nature

    b. Playing with friends

c. Baking a pie

d. Eating a pie

11. If you won a Thanksgiving lottery, what would be the prize?

    a. One million dollars

    b. One million turkeys

    c. One million pies

    d. One million Pilgrims

12. If you could pick a name for people to call you on Thanksgiving, what would it be?

    a. Turkey McTurkskins

    b. Pilgrim Priscilla

    c. Cherry Bob-ler

    d. Gary Gobbler

13. What do you think is the most difficult part of Thanksgiving day?

    a. Talking to your whole family

    b. Eating food until you're stuffed

    c. Finding room for dessert after dinner

    d. Having to run around on a full stomach

14. Which person at your Thanksgiving table would make the best television actor?

    a. Grandmother

    b. Grandfather

    c. Cousin

    d. Parents

15. If you had to wear a Thanksgiving-themed outfit every day, which would you choose?

    a. Turkey costume

b. Pilgrim clothes

c. Native America clothes

d. A fall sweater your grandmother knitted

16. What is the best way to use turkey leftovers?

   a. Bake into meat pies

   b. Freeze and eat later in the month

   c. Cook with eggs for breakfast

   d. What leftovers?!

17. If there was one thing that a family member could do to make your day, which would it be?

   a. Let you eat their pie

   b. Let you serve your plate ahead of them

   c. Tell you a cool story you've heard before

d. Teach you a new skill

18. If you could experience Thanksgiving in one of these decades, which would you choose?

    a. The 1600s (first Thanksgiving)

    b. The 1800s

    c. The 2000s

    d. The 2100s

19. If you could talk to one person from the original Thanksgiving, which would you choose?

    a. A pilgrim

    b. A Native American

    c. The person who cooked the food

    d. The person who ate the most food

20. Which thing would you make you smile the most on Thanksgiving day?

    a. Watching the parade on television

    b. Getting to see your grandparents

    c. Playing with your cousins and siblings

    d. Eating as much food as you can

21. If you could accomplish one of the listed things this year, which would it be?

    a. Make someone smile every day

    b. Earn twice the amount of money you did last year

    c. Make a new friend each month

    d. Help your parents more in the house

22. What are you most grateful for this year?

    a. Family

b. Education

c. Sports

d. New toys

23. What is the best compliment someone could give you at Thanksgiving dinner?

    a. You grew an inch!

    b. You're getting smarter every day.

    c. You finished your entire plate.

    d. You look just like your mother/father.

24. What is the best part of summer turning into fall?

    a. Weather gets cooler

    b. The leaves start falling

    c. Fall sports begin

    d. You can start eating pie

25. If you had to write a book report about your family's Thanksgiving tradition, what would be the title?

    a. Not-so-traditional traditions

    b. Just like the Pilgrims Did

    c. A Simple Kind of Holiday

    d. It Would Take Too Long to Explain...

Thanksgiving Funny Phrases

1. The (*adjective*) turkey walked across the street to the (*noun: place*) to buy some (*noun: thing*). He was hoping to use these in his Thanksgiving (*noun*) because he was having his entire (*noun*) over for (*noun*). When he entered the (*noun*), though, the (*noun*) caught his eye. They were (*adjective*), (*adjective*), and (*adjective*), but when he (*verb*) them they (*verb*). The turkey (*verb*) the only (*noun*) that wasn't (*adjective*), but a (*noun*) came over and (*verb*) at the turkey for (*verb*) his (*noun*) and kicked the turkey out of

his (*noun*). The turkey was so (*adjective*) that he (*verb*) all the way home.

2. The pilgrim (*verb*) at his friend on their (*noun*) because his hair was (*adjective*). Just then, a (*noun*) crested over the ship and (*verb*) them both. The two (*adjective*) pilgrims (*verb*) and searched for (*noun*), but those were (*adjective*) too. Then, they (*verb*) a (*adjective*) (*noun*) sitting on the deck. Before they could (*verb*), the (*noun*) lifted his (*noun*) and (*verb*) the Pilgrims. It (*verb*) the Pilgrims overboard and into the (*noun*) with the (*noun*). The Pilgrims had to (*verb*) to reach the (*noun*) and saw the (*noun*) (*verb*) their boat. They (*verb*) for it to (*verb*), but the (*noun*) didn't listen and (*verb*) away into the sunset.

3. Two (*adjective*) scarecrows (*verb*) in the yard and (*verb*). They were (*adjective*) and wished they could go (*noun*). One scarecrow (*verb*) and made it down off his perch. He (*verb*) at the other scarecrow and (*verb*) if he needed (*noun*). The second scarecrow, who was (*adjective*) and (*adjective*), couldn't (*verb*) on his own. So the first scarecrow (*verb*) him in the (*noun*) and (*verb*) over to a nearby

(*noun*) for some (*noun*). When he sat under the (*adjective*) (*noun*) and an (*noun*) fell on his head. He (*verb*) the apple and found (*noun*) inside of it. He'd rather sit in the sun than eat an (*noun*) with a (*adjective*) (*noun*) in it!

4. A farmer (*verb*) at his (*noun*) and thought about Thanksgiving. If he (*verb*) (*number*) (*noun*) and bought (*number*) turkey(s), then maybe he could (*verb*) a great (*noun*). So he (*verb*) to the (*noun*) and picked some (*adjective*) (*noun*), then (*verb*) to the (*noun*) and picked some (*noun*). That night he (*verb*) the (*adjective*) (*noun*) his family had ever seen. After the (*noun*), his daughter went (*place*) to check on the (*adjective*) (*noun*). When she saw the (*noun*) were (*verb*), she called her father for (*noun*). He couldn't tell her he'd (*verb*) the (*adjective*) (*noun*) so he said they (*verb*) because there was a (*adjective*) (*noun*) in the (*noun*).

5. The (*adjective*) kid wanted to (*verb*) (*noun*). He (*verb*) all his friends, but (*number*) of them said yes. So he (*verb*) to the (*adjective*) (*noun*) and began to (*verb*) the (*noun*). Then, one friend

offered to (*verb*) the ball so he could (*verb*) it. The (*adjective*) kid agreed, but when he (*verb*) to (*verb*) the ball he (*verb*) and (*verb*) on his (*adjective*) (*noun*). The other kid, who was (*adjective*) and (*adjective*), (*verb*) at the other boy for (*verb*). So instead of (*verb*) the (*noun*) the boy (*verb*) him! The (*adjective*) kid (*verb*) and (*verb*) all the way home to his mother.

6. Jimmy's (*adjective*) grandmother went to the (*noun*) for Thanksgiving dinner. When she (*verb*), she realized she'd (*verb*) her (*noun*) at home. So Jimmy (*verb*) (*adverb*) all the way to the (*noun*) and (*verb*) new (*noun*) for his grandmother. She didn't like them, though, so she (*verb*) at Jimmy until her face turned (*adjective*) and (*adjective*). Jimmy was (*adjective*) so he (*verb*) to the bathroom to get some (*noun*). When he came back with the (*noun*), his grandmother (*verb*) and would not take it. So he (*verb*) his (*adjective*) grandmother out of her (*noun*) and decided to (*verb*) for the rest of the day.

7. Thanksgiving dinner was only (*number*) days and (*name*) was so (*adjective*). He had been (*verb*) for an entire week to (*verb*) for the (*noun*). He was hoping for (*adjective*) casseroles and (*adjective*) turkey, but most of all for (*adjective*), (*adjective*), and (*adjective*) pies. When he arrived at his (*relative's*) house, he found all his (*noun*) had come true. There was (*adjective*) snacks, (*adjective*) casseroles, (*adjective*) turkey, ham, and chicken, and even (*adjective*) pies and cakes. He was so (*adjective*) that he (*told*) his (*aunt*) that he would (*verb*) every year to (*verb*) her food and even help her (*verb*) (*noun*) after.

8. The (adjective), (adjective) girl decided to dress up as a (noun) for Thanksgiving. She went to the (noun) and collected (noun), (noun), and (noun). When she returned home, she (verb) because the bag of (noun) had turned into a real (noun). The (noun) jumped out of the bag and began (verb) all over her (noun). She (verb) at the (adjective) (noun) and (verb) it. The (noun) was (adjective), though, and (verb) and (verb) around all of her

28

attempts. So finally, she had to (verb) to get the (noun) back in the bag. It was a (adjective) and (adjective) task, but she managed to (verb) with a little effort.

9. The (*person*) was in the kitchen (*verb*) dinner. (*Pronoun*) was making (*noun*) for the entire family, but she had run out of (*noun*). The (*noun*) was empty, and the (*adjective*) refrigerator was (*adjective*). All the (*noun*) were closed for the (*noun*). So she went (*place*) and (*verb*) until she found some (*noun*). The (*adjective*) (*noun*) smelled (*adjective*) and (*adjective*). So she (*thought*) for a moment, then (*verb*) to it anyway. The (*noun*), however, made her (*noun*) taste (*adjective*) and (*adjective*). All the (*noun*) refused to (*verb*) it, and there was a (*adjective*) (*noun*) of it left over for the next (*time period*).

10. After (*verb*) a giant (*noun*), the man decided to take a (*noun*). He (*verb*) on the (*noun*) in his (*noun*) until the sound of the (*noun*) made him get up. He (*verb*) out the window and saw (*number*) rows of (*noun*) marching in his yard. They were (*adjective*), (*adjective*), and (*adjective*),

which made his (*noun*) (*verb*). So he ran (*place*) to see who was leading the (*noun*) When he found the leader they (*verb*) and said the (*noun*) was supposed to be a (*noun*). The (*adjective*) man looked around and (*verb*) that they were obviously not a (*noun*). Then, he (*verb*) and realized it was all a (*noun*).

Chapter 2: Christmas and Winter

Who doesn't love the wintertime? Christmas is in the air and snow is on the ground, kids are out of school and there's joy all around! Winter is the perfect time to find new things you enjoy and make new friends along the way. This section includes the same types of games and questions as the previous one, but with a winter and Christmas theme. The would-you-rather questions are tough and silly and will make you think about a ton of different holiday scenarios. The questions will make you think about what your favorite parts of the season and then mad libs can give you some comedic relief after all that thinking. So enjoy this section while you keep an eye out for Santa or his reindeer!

Would You Rather...

1. Would you rather get a giant stocking full of candy or one large present?

2. Would you rather assist the elves in the workshop or train the reindeer during the off-season?

3. Would you rather make a snowman or a snow fort?

4. Would you rather spend Christmas with your mom's side of the family or your dad's side of the family?

5. Would you rather stand in as the family Christmas tree for a day or dress like an elf at school for a week?

6. Would you rather have Christmas lights for fingers or toes?

7. Would you rather spend an entire day playing in the snow but not be allowed to play in it again that week, or play in the snow for only one hour each day of the week?

8. Would you rather have to wait until the end of Christmas day to open presents and get all of your presents or open presents first thing in the morning, but you only get to choose one to open?

9. Would you rather help mom undecorate the Christmas tree or help dad shovel snow out of the driveway?

10. Would you rather start a snowball fight with your friends or end a snowball fight with your friends?

11. Would you rather give all of your friends one small present or give your best friend three large presents?

12. Would you rather listen to one Christmas carol on repeat for an entire week or only be allowed to listen to Christmas carols for an entire year?

13. Would you rather stay up and try to catch Santa, but risk not getting your presents, or go to sleep and let Santa be a mystery?

14. Would you rather wear your mittens on your feet or wear your socks on your hands?

15. Would you rather wear Christmas stockings instead of shoes to school or wear an elf's shirt instead of a regular shirt?

16. Would you rather have to sing everything you say for the month of December or not be able to speak for the entire week of Christmas?

17. Would you rather make Christmas cookies and not be allowed to eat them or be given a fruit cake and be allowed to eat it?

18. Would you rather live in an igloo or a gingerbread house?

19. Would you rather pick the Christmas tree, but not be the one to decorate it, or not pick the Christmas tree and you are the one who decorates it?

20. Would you rather decorate the house for Christmas, but none of your friends can come over, or not decorate the house and all of your friends can come over?

21. Would you rather go snowshoeing in the forest or snow skiing down a barren hill?

22. Would you rather trade your sled for a snowboard or your best present for a gift card?

23. Would you rather eat Christmas dinner every day for a month or eat soup every day for a year?

24. Would you rather play baseball in the snow or play hockey in the snow?

25. Would you rather figure skating in front of your friends or singing a Christmas carol?

26. Would you rather be a snowflake in a snowstorm or a snowball in a snowball fight?

27. Would you rather play in the snow with one of your siblings for a week or by yourself for a month?

28. Would you rather hide inside a snowman or a snow fort to scare someone?

29. Would you rather spend one whole year in winter or one whole year in summer?

30. Would you rather shovel the driveway of snow or pour salt on it afterward?

Christmas Jokes

1. What do you call a plant that scores the most points in a contest?

2. What do sheep say at Christmas?

3. What do reindeer decorate their antlers with?

4. What do you say when someone burns the Christmas dinner?

5. Where does Santa sleep during his gift delivery?

6. What do you call it when people become nostalgic during the holidays?

7. What does an elf use to make a sandwich?

8. If you were a shepherd, what would be the most delicious way to herd your sheep?

9. What does Frosty the Snowman need when he's sick?

10. What do you say when a Christmas situation gets stressful?

11. What do animals use for music during the holidays?

12. What kind of store does a reindeer visit for a new tail?

13. What happens when you run into a shark made of snow?

14. Why is Christmas the best time to make a mummy?

15. What do you call an amphibian covered in tinsel?

16. What did the gingerbread man use when he got cold?

17. Why is the turkey the most stylish bird?

18. What is Frosty's favorite fashion accessory?

19. How does Rudolph keep track of his schedule?

20. How do Eskimos repair their homes?

21. Why is the chimney Santa's favorite way to get into a house?

22. What is an elf's favorite type of music?

23. How did the elf ensure he'd sleep like a log?

24. Do residents of the north pole go to school?

25. What is Frosty the Snowman's favorite lunch?

Christmas and Winter Questions

1. What is your favorite outdoor activity when it's snowing?

    a. Snowboarding

    b. Sledding

    c. Snowball fight

    d. Capture the flag

2. What is your favorite part of Christmas?

    a. Presents

    b. Family

    c. Cookies

38

d. Hot chocolate

3. If you had a stable, how many reindeer would you own?

    a. 1

    b. 4

    c. 6

    d. 12

4. How do you think Santa gets into your home?

    a. The chimney

    b. The window

    c. The air vent

    d. The front door

5. What do you think is a reindeer's favorite snack?

a. Carrots

b. Candy canes

c. Christmas cookies

d. Milk

6. What is the best way to spend a snow day?

    a. Outside playing with friends

    b. Inside by the fire

    c. Building a snowman

    d. Making hot chocolate

7. What does Santa most likely do in the off-season?

    a. Spends time at his beach house

    b. Follows up on his naughty list

    c. Has a barbecue for the elves

    d. Goes surfing

8. What is your favorite part of getting a Christmas tree?

    a. Picking it out at the yard

    b. Putting it up in your house

    c. Stringing the lights around the tree

    d. Putting the ornaments on

9. What is your favorite winter holiday?

    a. Thanksgiving

    b. Christmas

    c. New Year's

    d. Valentine's Day

10. When is your ideal time to put up Christmas decorations?

    a. The day after Thanksgiving

    b. December 1st

c. The week before Christmas

d. You don't decorate your house

11. What is your favorite winter drink?

    a. Hot chocolate

    b. Apple cider

    c. Hot tea

    d. Warm milk

12. What is your favorite Christmas tradition?

    a. Gift giving

    b. Decorating the tree

    c. Dinner with family

    d. Opening stockings

13. What would be the first thing you did if you could go to the North Pole?

a. Meet Santa

b. Tour the workshop

c. Play with the reindeer

d. Have dinner with Mrs. Clause

14. If you could take a snow holiday and stay in any of the below places, which would you pick?

   a. A cabin in the woods

   b. An igloo

   c. A tent

   d. A hotel

15. What is your favorite thing about the winter?

   a. Snow

   b. Holidays

   c. Time away from school

d. Playing with friends

16. What would be the best present you could receive on Christmas Day?

    a. A new book

    b. A new video game

    c. A new sweater

    d. A new toy

17. If you could only make Christmas cookies in one shape, which would you choose?

    a. Reindeer

    b. Snowman

    c. Candy cane

    d. Ornament

18. Which day in the Christmas season do you like the most?

a. The first day off of school

b. Christmas Eve

c. Christmas Day

d. The day after Christmas

19. Which of the below is your favorite Christmas carol?

a. Jingle Bells

b. Santa Claus is Coming to Town

c. Silent Night

d. Oh Christmas Tree

20. If you could have any holiday mode of transportation, which would you choose?

a. The Polar Express

b. Santa's Sleigh

c. A reindeer

d. An elf's sled

21. What is your favorite type of gift to give other people?

    a. Handmade

    b. Books

    c. Movies

    d. Cards

22. Which thing would be least upset if you lost it?

    a. Mittens

    b. Scarf

    c. Socks

    d. Boots

23. How many times do you think Santa has gotten stuck in a chimney?

    a. 2

    b. 3

c. 6

d. 10

24. What is your grandmother most likely to give you for Christmas?

    a. Socks

    b. A sweater

    c. A book

    d. Your favorite toy

25. Who do you appreciate the most during the Christmas season?

    a. Your parents

    b. Your grandparents

    c. Your teachers

    d. Your coaches

Christmas and Winter Funny Phrases

1. A (*adjective*) and (*adjective*) snowman (*verb*) down the snowy mountain one day. When he reached the bottom he (*verb*) a (*adjective*) (*noun*). The (*noun*) seemed incredibly (*adjective*) so he (*verb*) and continued on his way. Next, he encountered a (*adjective*) (*noun*) that was (*verb*) in the trees. The (*adjective*) snowman went over to the (*noun*), but when he pulled away the branches he saw there were actually (*number*) of them! The snowman (*verb*) and tried to (*verb*), but the (*noun*) were not trying to (*verb*) him. That was when he realized they were not (*adjective*), but actually very (*adjective*) and (*adjective*).

2. Santa Clause looked in the mirror and saw his (*adjective*) belly and (*adjective*) cheeks and decided he was ready to join the gym. He filled out a (*noun*) at the North Pole gym and told the (*adjective*) attendant that he would start by (*verb*). Santa hopped on the (*noun*) and started to (*verb*). After a while, though, his face turned (*adjective*) and he felt (*adjective*).

He decided that was enough for one day. Santa (*verb*) in his sleigh and (*verb*) all the way back home to the North Pole where he sat and ate (*noun*) and drank (*noun*).

3. Rudolph was feeling (*adjective*) about his (*adjective*) nose. So he asked some (*noun*) what they thought about it. They (*verb*) at him and (*verb*). So Rudolph went to find more people to ask. He ran into some (*noun*) and they (*verb*) and told him his nose was (*adjective*). Rudolph still did not feel better, so he ran over to the (*noun*) where the rest of the (*noun*) (*verb*). When he arrived, they were all (*verb*) and didn't even (*verb*) when he came in. So he (*verb*) his (*adjective*) nose and got all of their attention right away.

4. The (*adjective*) elf walked into the (*noun*) to see all of his friends. When he arrived, he (*verb*) his friends all (*verb*) in one corner of the room. His (*adjective*) group of friends were picking names for a (*adjective*) contest. The elf (*verb*) and the others agreed to include him. He (*verb*) a name out of the hat and was (*adjective*) when he read it. It was the name of the

(*adjective*), (*adjective*) girl he had a crush on for (*number*) years. Now, he would be able to get her the (*adjective*) (*noun*) she had ever received and she might be so happy that she (*verb*) him.

5. Once upon a time, there was a (*adjective*), (*adjective*) snowflake. He enjoyed (*verb*) on the breeze and (*verb*) on the ground. His favorite time of year was (*season*) because all the (*noun*) would fill the air with (*adjective*) (*noun*). This year, however, when he (*verb*) down on the wind, the (*adjective*) snowflake didn't hear any (*noun*). He settled onto the (*adjective*) ground and realized that he kind of (*emotion*) the silence. So he sat until the (*noun*) came up over the trees and he began to (*verb*) in the silence of the (*adjective*) winter morning.

6. The (*adjective*) boy decided he wanted to go (*verb*) in the snow. He pulled on his (*noun*) and his (*noun*) and was ready to leave the (*adjective*) house when his mother stopped him. She said it was too (*adjective*) outside and he was not allowed to go (*verb*). The (*adjective*) boy sulked and (*verb*), but his mother did not

give in. When she walked away, the boy (*verb*) out the door and into the (*adjective*) snow. But the temperature was only (*number*) degrees and his (*body part*) quickly started turning (*color*). He (*verb*) back to his house where his (*adjective*) mother scolded him.

7. The (*adjective*) girl wanted to put up (*number*) ornaments on her Christmas tree. She had (*adjective*) ornaments and (*adjective*) ornaments and even (*adjective*) ornaments! She wanted to (*verb*) them all on her tree so it would look (*adjective*) and (*adjective*). Her brother, however, wanted to put (*noun*) on the tree instead. He said that (*noun*) were better than ornaments even though they weren't (*adjective*). The (*adjective*) girl ran to her mother and (*verb*). The mother came in and said they could each have (*fraction*) of the tree to (*verb*) any way they wanted.

8. As the (*adjective*) snow built up on the (*adjective*) (*noun*), the (*adjective*) child (*verb*) with his sled. He had been (*verb*) for the snow all year long, and now it was time to (*verb*). After putting on his (*noun*)

and (*noun*) he grabbed his (*color*) sled and (*verb*) outside into the cold. He (*verb*) on his sled and (*verb*) down the hill in a (*adjective*) race against time. His face was (*adjective*), his eyes were (*adjective*), and his heart was (*adjective*). When he finally hit the bottom of the (*noun*), he tumbled off his sled and landed in a (*adjective*) (*noun*).

9. The group of (*adjective*) Christmas carolers were traveling (*noun*) to (*noun*) to (*verb*) Christmas cheer and spirit. They (*verb*) on one (*noun*) and waited for someone to (*verb*). When they did, the (*adjective*) carolers would launch into prepared (*noun*) and hope the person would (*verb*) along. Sometimes the person who answered would (*verb*) and other times they seemed (*adjective*) and would (*verb*) the (*noun*) instead. The carolers could not be (*verb*), though, and they continued their (*route*) throughout the entire (*noun*). They were the only (*adjective*) group spreading Christmas (*noun*) and (*noun*) to people around them.

10. The lumberjack was (*emotion*) because every year he had to (*verb*) down (*adjective*) trees for people to put in their homes for Christmas. He, however, was (*adjective*) and loved nature, but he also needed (*noun*) to help his family. So each year, he (*verb*) and would (*verb*) trees until there were enough to sell to (*number*) farms in the town. When he was (*verb*) home one night, though, he (*verb*) one of his trees in the (*noun*) of a home. There were (*adjective*) children around it (*verb*) the lights and ornaments. That sight made him feel (*adjective*) about his job.

Chapter 3: New Year's

New Year's Eve is a holiday built around waiting, which isn't super fun when you're a kid. That's where this book can make your night waiting for the new year more fun than ever before. You can share the questions and would-you-rathers with friends and family who are waiting for midnight, or make it through the funny phrases to eat up time in a hilarious way. Any way you use this book, it is sure to get you through to the fireworks and big ball drop that signal a new year and a new beginning!

Would You Rather...

1. Would you rather throw a New Year's Eve party or attend one?

2. Would you rather attend the New Year's party in Times Square or attend a New Year's party at a celebrity's house?

3. Would you rather bring in the New Year with family or friends?

4. Would you rather be the curator of the fireworks show or be a spectator at the fireworks show?

5. Would you rather play games until midnight or talk to friends until midnight on New Year's Eve?

6. Would you rather stay up until midnight, but have to wake up at 6 a.m. or go to bed before midnight and get to wake up whenever you want?

7. Would you rather have sparklers or Roman candles?

8. Would you rather spend the night outside around a fire or inside watching television?

9. Would you rather your New Year's party be on local television or in the local newspaper?

10. Would you rather get to be famous on New Year's Day or get to meet someone famous?

11. Would you rather pay for all the food and fireworks at every New Year's Eve party

on your block or clean up all of Times Square by yourself on New Year's Day?

12. Would you rather spend New Year's in New York or Los Angeles?

13. Would you rather have to make 10 resolutions and stick to them all or make 100 resolutions but not have to follow them?

14. Would you rather eat an entire pot of party meatballs or drink the entire bowl of holiday punch?

15. Would you rather lose every game you play on New Year's Eve, but get to set off all the fireworks, or win every game and not get to light any fireworks?

16. Would you rather have to wear a winter hat every day for the next year or wear a scarf every day for the next year?

17. Would you rather only be able to tell people "Happy New Year" on New Year's Eve or have to say "Happy New Year" at every holiday for the next year?

18. Would you rather start a new year not knowing anything about the future or

reliving the past year knowing everything that's going to happen?

19. Would you rather skip ahead five years or go backward five years?

20. Would you rather clean your room every day for six months or not clean your room once for a year?

21. Would you rather get a new car every year or get a new house every year?

22. Would you rather be in charge of entertaining the children on New Year's Eve or the grandparents?

23. Would you rather have five years of bad luck, but you know when bad things will happen or have five years of good luck, but you don't know when good things will happen?

24. Would you rather relive the year of your favorite age or erase the year of your least favorite age?

25. Would you rather help set up for your New Year's party or help clean up your party?

26. Would you rather meet Father Time or your future self?

27. Would you rather watch a 10-minute firework show or play with sparklers all night long?

28. Would you rather bake the cookies for the party or decorate the cookies?

29. Would you rather spend the entirety of New Year's Eve indoors or outdoors?

30. Would you rather have the ability to see into the future or to fix the past for one minute on New Year's Day?

New Year's Jokes

1. What do jewelers do on New Year's Eve?

2. What is the most mathematical place on New Year's Eve?

3. How did the farmer show affection for his wife on New Year's Eve?

4. Why does the person who runs Times Square on New Year's Eve have low self-esteem?

5. What resolution did the man, who thought about the ways he could exercise more next year, make?

6. Why did the girl put candy under her pillow before going to bed on New Year's Eve?

7. What do you call a firework that doesn't explode?

8. What do you call someone who shows up on New Year's Eve Party at 12:01?

9. What did the man call it when he resolved to make more money next year?

10. Why do birds fly south for New Year's?

11. What did the man get who was caught for stealing a calendar?

12. Why did the boy want to put his new calendar in the freezer?

13. What do snowmen do for their New Year's Eve parties?

14. Which is more difficult to catch on New Year's Eve, heat or cold?

15. How do you begin the New Year in a good way?

16. What do you say when someone didn't listen to their own resolutions?

17. What's one clever way to follow a resolution to read more?

18. What do corn call the end of the year holiday?

19. What is your TV's resolution for New Year's?

20. What did the boxer say after he lost the match on New Year's Eve?

21. What is the difference between an optimist on New Year's and a pessimist?

22. Why would someone heat up bread just before midnight on New Year's Eve?

23. What do you call it when Dracula falls on New Year's Eve?

24. What is the biggest con of celebrating New Year's?

25. What resolution did the firework make?

New Year's Questions

1. Where would you want to attend a New Year's Eve party?

    a. A friend's house

    b. A family member's house

    c. A celebrity's house

    d. The White House

2. If you could pick any age to be next year, which would you pick?

    a. 12

    b. 16

    c. 25

    d. 40

3. What resolution would your friend make for you?

    a. Clean your room every day

b. Read one book every month

c. Pick up two extra chores a week

d. Give up your phone on weekdays

4. What would be the most fun way to spend New Year's Eve?

   a. Playing games

   b. Solving riddles

   c. Watching movies

   d. Popping fireworks

5. If you could get one wish on New Year's Eve, what would it be?

   a. Relive the past year

   b. Skip ahead one year

   c. Live the same week five times

   d. Only experience every other day

6. What is one school subject you wish would disappear next year?

    a. Math

    b. English

    c. History

    d. Art

7. What was your favorite activity this past year?

    a. Reading

    b. Watching television

    c. Playing sports

    d. Learning a new skill

8. What is your favorite snack at a New Year's Party?

    a. Meatballs

    b. Chips and dip

c. Cookies

d. Brownies

9. What green vegetable would you rather eat to ensure you'll get money in the new year?

    a. Cabbage

    b. Kale

    c. Spinach

    d. Collards

10. What is one thing you can spend more time doing next year?

    a. Reading

    b. Hanging out with friends

    c. Focusing on school

    d. Practicing sports

11. If you had to pick one person to spend New Year's with, who would you choose?

    a. Your grandmother

    b. Your grandfather

    c. Your best friend

    d. One of your siblings

12. What's the best part of being your age?

    a. The grade you're in

    b. An increase in allowance

    c. More adult responsibility

    d. You can cook your own food

13. If you had to turn into an animal after midnight, which would you choose?

    a. Leopard

    b. Giraffe

    c. Rhinoceros

d. Monkey

14. If you had to keep one resolution, which
    would you choose?

    a. Clean the house every week

    b. Do one outside chore a week

    c. Read a book each month

    d. Do your homework every night

15. If you could go back in time, which
    decade's New Year's party would you
    want to attend?

    a. 1600s

    b. 1800s

    c. 2000s

    d. 2100s

16. What is your favorite New Year's Eve
    drink?

a. Soda

b. Fruit punch

c. Water

d. Sparkling cider

17. If you could give yourself one piece of advice for the past year, what would it be?

   a. Don't worry about what your friends think

   b. Study more for that big test

   c. Practice extra to get better at sports

   d. Help your parents more

18. How would you prefer to celebrate the new year at midnight?

   a. Popping fireworks

   b. Singing karaoke with your friends

   c. Eating snacks

d. Playing card games

19. What would you rather do on New Year's Eve?

    a. Make 100 resolutions

    b. Clean the whole house after your party

    c. Eat all the snacks by yourself

    d. Drink all the fruit punch by yourself

20. If you had to sing the national anthem at a sporting event, which would you choose?

    a. A professional football game

    b. An international soccer game

    c. A high school hockey game

    d. The Olympics

21. What you prefer to buy if you knew you would win the lottery in the new year?

    a. A car

    b. A new house

    c. Clothes

    d. A new phone

22. What is your favorite type of holiday punch?

    a. Tooty Fruity

    b. Lemon-lime

    c. Berries and cream

    d. Sherbet float

23. What would you be your ideal New Year's Eve job?

    a. The news anchor in Times Square

    b. The person who drops the ball in Times Square

c. The person who sets off a fireworks show

d. The performer singing at midnight

24. If you had to pick one, which social media would you give up for the new year?

a. Snapchat

b. Netflix

c. Instagram

d. Facebook

25. How many resolutions do you usually keep after New Year's?

a. 0

b. 1

c. 2

d. 3

New Year's Funny Phrases

1. The (*adjective*) boy was so (*emotion*) for New Year's Eve. This was the first year he was allowed to (*verb*) at the party. He was (*emotion*) to show everyone his (*noun*) and have all eyes on him. When his time came, though, he felt (*adjective*) and (*adjective*). He grabbed the (*noun*) and started his performance. The more he (*verb*) the more comfortable he felt. When he was finished, the entire audience (*verb*) (*adverb*) and gave him a standing (*noun*). The (*adjective*) boy was so proud that he (*verb*) and performed a (*adjective*) encore for the (*adjective*) crowd.

2. The (*adjective*) ball was waiting for (*time*). He never liked (*noun*) or (*noun*) so the fact that they (*verb*) him every year was positively (*emotion*). As the clock counted down, he grew more and more (*emotion*), the waiting making him (*adjective*) and (*adjective*). When the man came to pull the (*noun*), the ball braced for impact. All the people started (*verb*) in the square, and it knew it was

almost (*time*). They crowd yelled (*number*) and the person pulled the (*noun*) and the ball (*verb*) down to the ground. It made him so (*feeling*) that he released tons of (*noun*) all over the (*adjective*) crowd.

3. There were (*number*) celebrities in line to (*verb*) for New Year's Eve. The first celebrity was a (*noun*), and they were excited to showcase their skill, (*verb*). When they got on stage the (*adjective*) crowd (*verb*) and the celebrity (*verb*) their skill. The second celebrity was (*emotion*) because it was their (*number*) time ever being on stage. The (*adjective*) crowd met them with (*noun*) and (*noun*). The third celebrity was (*adjective*) and (*adjective*) and nothing made him feel (*emotion*). The fourth celebrity, however, was (*adjective*) and when they got on stage they (*verb*) all their lines. The (*adjective*) crowd (*verb*) and (*verb*) until the celebrity left.

4. There was once a (*adjective*) grandfather clock, who tick and tocked. It was New Year's Eve when this (*adjective*) clock thought it was time to (*verb*). So he

gathered up his (*noun*) and was ready to go, but the time was moving so (*adverb*). He waited and he (*verb*), but he was (*adjective*) and (*emotion*). The clock saw a (*noun*) sitting on the couch and thought it might be able to (*verb*) and help the time move (*adverb*). The (*adjective*) (*noun*), however, did not (*verb*) the clock when he chimed and dinged, so the (*adjective*) clock was stuck waiting for (*time*).

5. All the parents were (*location*) and the children were left (*location*) to play with their (*noun*). The (*adjective*) children were having fun playing (*noun*) and (*verb*). Everything was going well until one (*adjective*) boy broke the (*noun*). All the children (*verb*) and felt (*emotion*), but they tried to (*verb*) anyway. The boy felt so (*emotion*) about breaking the (*noun*), that he ran home to grab his (*noun*). When he returned, all the kids were so (*emotion*) to see him they (*verb*) and (*verb*) and played with the new (*noun*) for the rest of the night.

6. A group of (*adjective*) friends were at a New Year's Eve (*noun*). They had all

arrived together but were now looking to meet new (*noun*). The (*noun*) was ticking through the night, getting ever closer to (*time*). The (*adjective*) friends were all (*verb*) and (*verb*) with the new people at the party when they realized it was almost New Year's Day. They each grabbed a (*adjective*) (*noun*) and started to (*verb*) and count down from (*number*). As the time ticked by, it was finally midnight and the whole party (*verb*).

7. Father time was feeling (*emotion*) on New Year's Eve. He loved the holiday but wanted more (*noun*) involved. He (*verb*) and a solution came to him: he would (*verb*) time and watch the (*adjective*) people ponder about why the new year wasn't coming. He (*verb*) and got to work on his plan. He gathered up (*noun*), (*noun*), and (*noun*) and (*verb*) them in a (*noun*). An (*adjective*) (*noun*) started to (*verb*) in the container. As he added more things, time slowed and then (*verb*). All the (*adjective*) people were pondering and (*verb*) and no one knew why midnight wouldn't come.

8. The counter was set with (*adjective*) snacks and (*adjective*) drinks, all ready for the New Year's (*noun*). The (*emotion*) children couldn't wait to be allowed to dig in. There were in (*adjective*) cookies to (*verb*), and (*adjective*) sandwiches to (*verb*), and even (*adjective*) punch to (*verb*). They had been waiting (*time period*) for the (*noun*) to start, but the time was moving too slowly. So one child snuck into the (*place*) to steal a couple of (*noun*). As soon as he (*verb*) one of the snacks, though, his (*person*) was staring at him over the counter. He was (*noun*) and didn't eat any more (*adjective*) (*noun*) for the rest of the night.

9. It was (*time*) on New Year's night and the (*adjective*) dog had no intention of going to sleep. He'd seen the people (*verb*) and (*verb*) all night long and wanted to know what the fuss was about. The (*adjective*) people were all gathering outside, (*noun*) in hand, so he (*verb*). They began to count down from (*number*) and (*verb*) and (*verb*). When they made it to one, everyone (*verb*) and they all looked like (*adjective*) (*noun*). Next, the sky began to

(*verb*) with (*noun*). It was lit up (*adjective*) colors that the dog couldn't even see. He was (*emotion*) he stayed up to see the show.

10. The (*adjective*) firework was so (*emotion*) for New Year's he could barely contain it. She wanted (*verb*) in the sky more (*adverb*) than any other firework ever had. She had been (*verb*) all (*time period*) for this moment. All she needed was a (*noun*) and a (*noun*) and she would be ready to go. The (*adjective*) colors she would produce would make all the (*adjective*) people feel (*emotion*) and (*verb*). A person was (*verb*) with a light in his hand, and she (*verb*). It was time. He lit her end and she (*verb*) into the sky and was the most (*adjective*) (*noun*) anyone saw that whole night.

Chapter 4: Joke Answers

Thanksgiving

1. he wanted mashed potatoes
2. to run away from Thanksgiving dinner
3. an apple gobbler
4. so they don't fall off
5. they're prone to fowl play
6. wobble, wobble
7. Plymouth Rock
8. he has berry treasure
9. the drums because he has drum sticks
10. because they like to gobble
11. they're stuffed
12. husky
13. they hugged the coast
14. a har-vest
15. your nose
16. of course; skyscrapers can't fly!
17. Cinna-mon
18. Pal-grim
19. a tur-key
20. his age
21. the chef lost track of thyme
22. pi

23. a Butter Ball
24. it sneezed
25. an arrow escape

Christmas

1. a point-setter (Poinsettia)
2. "Merry Christmas to Ewe"
3. horn-aments
4. Merry Crispness
5. a ho-ho-hotel
6. Santa-mental
7. shortbread
8. with a giant candy cane
9. a chill pill
10. this is in-tinsel
11. jungle bells
12. re-tail stores
13. frostbite
14. there's tons of extra wrapping
15. mistle-toad
16. cookie sheet
17. it's always well-dressed
18. an ice cap
19. by looking at a calen-deer
20. with ig-glue
21. it "soots" him best
22. wrap music

23. he moved his bed to the fireplace
24. No, they're all "elf" taught
25. ice-bergers

New Year's

1. ring in the new year
2. Times Square-d
3. with hogs and kisses
4. because he always drops the ball
5. to stop thinking
6. she wanted sweet dreams
7. a sparkler
8. late to the party
9. reso-loot-ion
10. it's too far to walk
11. 12 months
12. to start the new year in a cool way
13. chill out
14. heat, because it's easy to catch a cold
15. start it on your right foot
16. It went in one year and out the other
17. put subtitles on the TV
18. New Ear's Day
19. 1080p
20. "I needed more holiday punch!"
21. one greets the new year and the other waits for the old one to leave

22. to make a toast
23. a Count down
24. con-fetti
25. to start the new year with a bang

Conclusion

How did you like the book? Hopefully, you found one section that was undoubtedly your favorite. Maybe you even found sections that you want to go back to and try again. That's the beauty of this book! It's never out of surprises or new areas for you to explore.

Keep in mind, you don't have to keep the fun only to the holiday season. You can take this book out at any time of the year when you want to have a little fun. It can also be great for those days when you're missing cool weather and family gatherings. The holiday-themed scenarios can bring you back to the time you're missing.

As an extra challenge, you can even pull this book out in the summertime and see if you can adapt the activities. See if you can turn winter would-you-rathers into summertime stumpers. See if you can make Thanksgivings jokes into swimming hole humor.

If you absolutely loved this book, keep an eye out for other exciting activity books by this author. You can keep the fun going all year round with crazy questions, crazy questions, and silly situations that will make your head spin. Celebrate every season with the best activities around!

Don't Gather Dust

Once you've made it through the whole book once, don't let it gather dust on the shelf. There are tons of ways you can use this book every day in every way to get the maximum amount of fun out of the activities. All you have to do is use a little imagination and the possibilities will seem endless!

You can use it as a guide to make your own riddles and games throughout the year if you want to try your hand at coming with jokes specifically tailored to you. Use subjects such as your classes, clubs, or sports to focus on when thinking up questions. You can even use something funny that happened to you to make a wacky word game.

Another fun way to use the book is to see if you can find activities hidden in the sections of this book. Maybe a would-you-rather about baking or decorating cookies was hard to choose. Try baking some cookies then decorating them to see which you enjoyed more. Don't let the words end on the page, put them to action!

If there were any sections that seemed particularly easy or hard, go back to them and try them again. See if your answers have changed since the last time you tried the questions. The easy questions might seem more difficult than they originally did, and the harder questions might be easier to figure out the second time around.

You can even use this book as inspiration to get into the holiday spirit. Sometimes, when the seasons roll around, it can be easy to get caught up in school and sports and forget to feel the magic in the air. As the air starts to grow colder, use this book to start setting your mind to holiday time.

Share with Friends

Everyone likes to enjoy a fun new activity, so be sure to share this book with your friends and family. Although it is geared toward kids who are between the ages of 9 and 12, anyone of any age can find something fun to do in these pages. So don't be shy to invite others in on the fun!

You can bring it to school with you to practice your skills with friends during recess or at lunchtime. You can even use it as a way to pass the time on the bus in the morning or afternoon. If you want to make a new friend, using the would-you-rather or multiple-choice questions can be a great way to break the ice. You can also show it to your teacher and ask for him or her to let the whole class play. In the last few days before the holiday break, they might be willing to make some time for a little fun. Then you can be the hero who got the class out of busy work!

It can also be a great way to meet new people at a new club or sport. Being the new kid can be scary, but when you're equipped with jokes to make everyone laugh, you'll be able to fit in right away. Once you've made a few friends, you can even loan them the book to see how quickly they can make their way through it. Challenge them with a deadline and then check how many answers they got right or how many match yours.

Try It All Again!

Once you've shared the fun with friends, don't be afraid to go and do it all over again! You can pull in family members to go through it with you to see what answers other people come up with and who is smart enough to guess the answer to a joke on a first try.

Would-you-rather questions always have a different answer, whether you ask other people or you go through them again yourself. The jokes can be new to anyone you meet, so try to memorize a few and make people laugh at school. As you get older the answers to your questions might change. For this reason, it can be fun to circle your answers in pencil so you can go back and change them as you grow. Finally, the wacky situations have never-ending potential to be a hilariously different story every time you play. Keep lists of your favorite words to share with friends.

Made in the USA
Monee, IL
30 December 2022

24083674R00059